This is a must have field guide for every leader written by the man who has seen every scenario, condition, and obstacle you are facing in the mountains ahead. **Todd Adkins - Director of LifeWay Leadership**

Will normalizes the natural reactions that occur when one is considering retirement, both the joys as well as the concerns that they may not even be willing to name. *Embracing Succession* will be the greatest gift you can give to you yourself, your church, or organization in a season of transition. **Dana Allin - Synod Executive ECO: A Covenant Order of Evangelical Presbyterians**

Pastor, you've served with intentionality. If it's nearing time to transition into your next phase of life and ministry, *Embracing Succession* can help you be just as intentional. **Paul Chitwood - President of the International Mission Board (IMB)**

Will Heath offers the most biblically-based leadership succession planning that I have seen to date. **Ray Gentry - President/CEO of the Southern Baptist Conference of Associational Leaders**

Embracing Succession lays out essential issues to consider, gives insights from leaders who have navigated the waters of transition, and provides important questions to consider for those facing transition. **Kevin Komplien - President of the Evangelical Free Church of America**

Embracing Succession opens the door to both a candid and caring path to honor the past but embrace the future. The stories of individual journeys are personal, practical and powerful. **Scott Ridout - President of Converge**

Embracing Succession

HELPING MINISTRY LEADERS
CONFRONT THE PERSONAL SIDE OF
TRANSITION

Will Heath

CrossLink Publishing
RAPID CITY, SD

Heath/CrossLink Publishing
1601 Mt. Rushmore Rd., Ste 3288
Rapid City, SD 57701
www.CrossLinkPublishing.com

Ordering Information:
Quantity sales. Special discounts are available on quantity purchases by corporations, associations, and others. For details, contact the "Special Sales Department" at the address above.

Embracing Succession/Will Heath. —1st ed.
ISBN 978-1-63357-351-2
Library of Congress Control Number: 2020943951

To Steve . . . Thanks for lunch!

Some retiring leaders know who their successor will be. Others do not. Regardless of your context, you can lend your influence to prepare the people for what it looks like to follow someone else's lead. To not do so would be selfish and short-sighted.

—WILL HEATH

Contents

Foreword

by Bob Russell

Every church should develop a practical transition plan. Especially as a pastor nears retirement age, wise church leaders should initiate a workable method by which the baton can be smoothly passed to the next generation. What happens to the church when the preacher retires? What happens if he gets hit by a bus? Has a stroke and is incapacitated? Who will fill the pulpit? Lead the staff? Cast the vision? Guide decisions? Shepherd the flock? Regardless of the size of the congregation, good spiritual leaders see the wisdom of having a tentative transition plan for three reasons.

First, there is biblical precedent for it. Moses trained Joshua for forty years. David selected his son Solomon to succeed him. Elijah mentored Elisha, and Paul appointed

Timothy as his understudy. Paul wrote, "And the things you have heard me say in the presence of many witnesses entrust to reliable people who will also be qualified to teach others" (2 Timothy 2:2). Mentoring a successor and preparing to make a smooth transition of leadership is a consistent biblical principle.

A second reason for implementing a transition plan is the practical example that has been set by the business world. In recent years, major corporations are giving more and more attention to succession planning because they've seen businesses rise and fall on the CEO's strength. Analysts have witnessed how quickly a company can fall apart when it isn't prepared for its leader's departure, and they are sounding a warning. To develop consistent success for generations to come, executive boards are now thinking long term.

In his best-selling book *Built to Last*, Jim Collins, a popular business guru, has an entire section on mentoring. He writes, "Do not fall into the trap of thinking that the only way to bring about change and progress at the top is to bring in outsiders, who might dilute or destroy the core. The key is to develop and promote insiders who are highly capable of stimulating healthy change and progress while preserving the core."

Jesus said, "The children of darkness are often wiser in dealing with their own kind than are the children of light" (Luke 16:8). In other words, the secular world will often do more to make money than Christians do to advance God's kingdom. That should not be! If the topic of transition is vital in the business world, how much more important should it be in the kingdom of God?

The third reason for a church to seriously consider a transition plan is that common sense demands it. Imagine that a wealthy tycoon offers to pay you $100,000 to transport his car and his two young children from Boston to Los Angeles. There's just one catch: the car and the precious cargo have to be delivered in forty-eight hours. You'd probably leap at the opportunity; however, you wouldn't just jump in the car and immediately start a forty-eight-hour journey. Common sense tells you that you need a second driver. You know it would be nearly impossible to stay awake for two straight days. You'd get miserably sleepy and driving by yourself would become too dangerous, so you would find an associate driver to take over for you when you got weary.

The Lord has entrusted the leadership of his church to your care. Your responsibility is to deliver God's children to the eternal promised land. Common sense acknowledges that you can't fulfill that role alone. The body soon ages, the mind gets fuzzy, and the spirit is weak. Wisdom should motivate you to mentor a successor and prepare to pass the baton at the appropriate time so the entire congregation can make it safely to the promised land. If you really love the people God entrusted to your ministry (and are not just on an ego trip), then as surely as you buy life insurance to provide for your family when you're gone, you should be preparing someone to fill your leadership role in your absence.

Will Heath is especially equipped to address this critical subject. Will has studied the history of scores of churches and interviewed dozens of pastors about succession planning. He has conducted numerous surveys and analyzed both successful and botched transitions.

He has lectured on the subject and helped hundreds of pastors navigate their transition plans. I'm not aware of anyone who has done a more thorough study of succession than Will Heath.

In this book, Will uses Moses's encounter with God at Mount Pisgah as the basis for developing a biblical philosophy of transitions. Pisgah was where God prepared Moses for passing the leadership baton on to Joshua. Moses had to face the fact that he was not going to be around much longer, and he needed to take the necessary steps to prepare his understudy to take over.

Pisgah forces leaders to face their own mortality. Pisgah motivates leaders to swallow their egos and consider their people above themselves. Pisgah reminds us that when we are taken out of the way, the work of God continues.

The Lord said to Moses, "Go up to the top of Pisgah and lift up your eyes westward and northward and southward and eastward, and look at it with your eyes, for you shall not go over this Jordan. But charge Joshua, and encourage and strengthen him, for he shall go over at the head of this people, and he shall put them in possession of the land that you shall see" (Deuteronomy 3:27-28).

Introduction

I'll never forget my very first observation related to the topic of succession planning.

In 2007, I was having lunch with Steve, an older pastor of a church in a neighboring community. Steve was not only the pastor of the First Baptist Church, but he was also the chaplain to the police department, the fire department, and the high school football team. Every politician wanted his endorsement. Many of the young pastors in the area found their way to his office, looking for advice and encouragement. During his tenure, he had become the benevolent, spiritual godfather to an entire community. To me, however, he was just Steve . . . my friend and mentor.

In the week before one of our many lunch appointments, I had finished reading John Maxwell's *21 Laws of Leadership*. The twenty-first law, the "Law of Legacy," made me consider Steve. A few days later, we were at lunch. We sat down and spent the first few minutes of our meeting catching up and ordering food. Once we settled into the conversation, I gave him the book. He had not read it. I provided an overview of the Law of Legacy and asked him two questions.

1. *What will it look like for you to be "a pastor" when you are no longer "the pastor"?*

2. *How will the church maintain influence in the community when you are no longer the pastor?*

I had struck a nerve that, as a thirty-year-old, I didn't even realize existed. Over the next two hours, Steve shared the deep sense of anxiety he felt about this very issue. It was like I became the release valve for the pressure that had been building for some time. Until that point, I was the only person he had shared these thoughts and feelings with. The conversation was personal and left a deep mark in my soul. Walking away from that lunch meeting, I felt the Lord impress me to help Steve . . . and the thousands of other pastors and ministry leaders just like him.

It was in this lunch meeting that I learned my first lesson related to succession.

> **Succession planning is personal long before it becomes tactical.**

Since that lunch with Steve in 2007, the personal side of succession has become a primary filter for how I relate to ministry leaders contemplating a transition.

I like what Marshall Goldsmith wrote in his book, *Succession, Are You Ready?*: "'Academic' literature generally ignores the fact that CEOs—and their successors—are human beings. Very little of what is written deals with the 'soft' personal issues like relationships, self-interest, ego, or (God forbid) feelings!" (Preface: Memo to the CEO, page XIV).

Mr. Goldsmith's book is written to those in the C-suite of corporate America, but his comments apply to leaders in both secular and sacred organizations.

I wrote *Embracing Succession* to help pastors and ministry leaders reflect on those "soft, personal issues" that often go unaddressed. Moses's transition will be our primary reference:

> Go up to the top of Pisgah and lift up your eyes westward and northward and southward and eastward, and look at it with your eyes. (Deuteronomy 3:27 ESV)

Pisgah is the physical location God used to bring Moses to recognize it was time to appoint his successor. I use Moses's journey on that mountain as a metaphor for how leaders navigate the process of embracing a retirement-based transition.

Every leader will be confronted by their own personal Pisgah. At that moment, they will have the opportunity to reimagine the application of their calling for a new season. I pray this resource encourages you to embrace the journey.

Embracing Succession is organized into four sections.

Section 1 walks through the four principles related to Pisgah. Use the space provided at the end of each section to capture any thoughts or questions that come to mind.

Section 2 highlights the stories of five pastors I have had the privilege to work with. You will be encouraged and challenged to see the four principles outlined in Section 1 come alive.

Section 3 offers questions for couples contemplating a transition to process together.

Section 4 offers suggestions to consider as you continue your journey.

SECTION 1

Numbers 27:12–23 and Deuteronomy 3:23–28 are the primary biblical texts referenced throughout *Embracing Succession*. These are parallel passages that give us two different perspectives of the same conversation between God and Moses. Numbers 27 reveals the genuine concern Moses has for the people. The Deuteronomy passage gives us a peek into just how difficult this process was for him.

> The LORD said to Moses "Go up into this mountain of Abarim and see the land that I have given to the people of Israel. When you have seen it, you also shall be gathered to your people, as your brother Aaron was, because you rebelled against my

word in the wilderness of Zin when the congregation quarreled, failing to uphold me as holy at the waters before their eyes." (These are the waters of Meribah of Kadesh in the wilderness of Zin.) Moses spoke to the LORD, saying, "Let the LORD, the God of the spirits of all flesh, appoint a man over the congregation who shall go out before them and come in before them, who shall lead them out and bring them in, that the congregation of the LORD may not be as sheep that have no shepherd." So the LORD said to Moses, "Take Joshua the son of Nun, a man in whom is the Spirit, and lay your hand on him. Make him stand before Eleazar the priest and all the congregation, and you shall commission him in their sight. You shall invest him with some of your authority, that all the congregation of the people of Israel may obey. And he shall stand before Eleazar the priest, who shall inquire for him by the judgment of the Urim before the LORD. At his word they shall go out, and at his word they shall come in, both he and all the people of Israel with him, the whole congregation." And Moses did as the LORD commanded him. He took Joshua and made him stand before Eleazar the priest and the whole congregation, and he laid his hands on him and commissioned him as the LORD directed through Moses. (Numbers 27:12-23 ESV)

"And I pleaded with the LORD at that time, saying, 'O LORD God, you have only begun to show your servant your greatness and your mighty hand. For what god is there in heaven or on earth who can do such works and mighty acts as yours? Please let me go over and see the good land beyond the Jordan, that good hill country and Lebanon.' But the LORD was angry with me because of you and would not listen to me. And the LORD said to me, 'Enough from you; do not speak to me of this matter again. Go up to the top of Pisgah and lift up your eyes westward and northward and southward and eastward, and look at it with your eyes, for you shall not go over this Jordan. But charge Joshua, and encourage and strengthen him, for he shall go over at the head of this people, and he shall put them in possession of the land that you shall see.'" (Deuteronomy 3:23-28 ESV)

We will use these passages to illustrate the following principles related to retirement-based transitions:

Principle 1: Pisgah represents a shift, not an end.

Principle 2: The road to Pisgah is emotional.

Principle 3: Pisgah forces the leader to consider the needs of the people.

Principle 4: Pisgah forces the leader to consider the successor.

Pisgah Represents a Shift, Not an End

Pisgah marked a profound shift in how Moses understood what it meant for him to lead the nation. Climbing Pisgah, Moses's primary leadership objective was to lead Israel to the promised land. Coming down from Pisgah, his primary focus had shifted to prepare the nation and his successor for the day he was longer with them.

In western, capitalistic culture, retirement is often seen as a finish line. Like Steve, few ministry leaders have thought of what it means to be "a pastor" when they are no longer "the pastor." The unfortunate consequence is that leaders tend to contextualize their life-long calling exclusively through the lens of a defined position within an organizational structure. It is no wonder why aging leaders struggle to understand what it looks like to have significant, ongoing contributions after they have transitioned.

Almost four decades before climbing Pisgah, God gave Moses instructions on managing the reality of an aging Levite workforce.

> And the LORD spoke to Moses, saying, "This applies to the Levites: from twenty-five years old and upward they shall come to do duty in the service of the tent of meeting. And from the age of fifty years they shall withdraw from the duty of the service and serve no more. They minister to their brothers in the tent of meeting by keeping guard, but they shall do no service. Thus shall you do to the Levites in assigning their duties." (Numbers 8:23–26 ESV)

Levites from ages twenty-five to fifty were responsible for managing the day-to-day activities related to the Tent of Meeting. At the age of fifty, there was a mandatory transition of function. It wasn't that the fifty-year-old Levite was no longer necessary or wanted; it was simply that their role had shifted. They moved from being accountable for the work to being responsible to the workers.

Even though this rule regarding the Levites didn't specifically apply to Moses, I believe the concept did. He was an aging leader who needed to address the topic of succession. Pisgah marked the moment when Moses finally owned the reality that his role needed to shift. God made it clear that the time had come for him to prepare the people and his successor. But even though it was time for his succession, he was not a lame duck.

Consider this. Joshua was named Moses's successor at the end of Numbers 27 and at the end of Deuteronomy 3. The book of Numbers has thirty-six chapters. The book of Deuteronomy has thirty-four. Moses is still leading and influencing the nation after Joshua was named his successor. He is reminding Israel of its past and recounting the faithfulness of God. He teaches laws and statutes while encouraging the people to trust and obey the Lord as they move forward. He is leading, even though his role has shifted.

There comes a point in every ministry leader's life when their most significant contribution and platform of influence shifts from the performance of tasks to protection and mentoring. The Levites' responsibility shifted from production in the tabernacle to protecting the others. Moses's leadership moved from leading the people into Canaan to preparing the people and Joshua.

Here are specific ways this shift has played out with ministry leaders I have worked with:

- One pastor realized his greatest contribution was no longer the sermons he preached, but in coaching younger pastors to communicate more effectively.

- One pastor realized his most effective role wasn't to lead the next strategic initiative but to cheer on and support his successor as he drove it.

- One visible pastor began to intentionally reduce his time in the spotlight, choosing to stand in the shadows and help younger leaders understand how to avoid the traps of spiritual influence.

- One pastor realized his contribution was no longer tied to shepherding the people within his congregation, but in partnering with a local seminary to encourage and train younger ministry leaders.

Please understand, I am not saying that older leaders shouldn't preach, spearhead strategic initiatives, be visible, or lead an organization. However, Pisgah forces a leader to reimagine how they will implement their pastoral calling in their next season of influence.

Moses continued to lead after coming down from Pisgah, but in a different way.

Pastor Randy, one of the stories highlighted in Section 2, benefited from succeeding a pastor that embraced Pisgah. Upon retirement, Pastor Bruce stayed involved in the church and became Randy's biggest cheerleader, advocate, friend, and ministry supporter. Embracing his new role gave Bruce an incredible amount of satisfaction and purpose after he shifted roles. His posture also inspired Randy to do the same for his successor.

Be encouraged, but take heed. Pisgah represents a shift, not an end. Succession *planning* (notice the emphasis) doesn't fully take place until a leader begins to embrace Pisgah's reality. It is heartbreaking to watch leaders refuse to acknowledge when their current season has ended. In these situations, other ministry leaders are forced to begin navigating what is functionally a glorified termination. This is frustrating to observe, gut-wrenching to experience, and completely avoidable.

Use the space below to record any thoughts or questions you have about your eventual "shift."

The Road to Pisgah Is Emotional

Succession is personal long before it becomes tactical. The Deuteronomy passage below provides insight into the emotion that Moses worked through.

> And I pleaded with the Lord at that time, saying, "O LORD God, you have only begun to show your servant your greatness and your mighty hand. For what god is there in heaven or on earth who can do such works and mighty acts as yours? Please let me go over and see the good land beyond the Jordan, that good hill country and Lebanon." But the LORD was angry with me because of you and

> would not listen to me. And the LORD said to me, "Enough from you; do not speak to me of this matter again." (Deuteronomy 3:23–26 ESV)

Moses had been the leader of Israel for almost forty years at this point. Some years before this moment (we are not sure of the exact timeline), Moses had made a mistake. His sister had just died. The people were frustrated, hungry, and thirsty. Fueled by a high level of momentary frustration, Moses was flippant in handling the situation. Unlike so many sins and mistakes that had been forgiven, this one would not be overlooked. Here is God's response (read the full account in Numbers 20:1–13):

> And the Lord said to Moses and Aaron, "Because you did not believe in me, to uphold me as holy in the eyes of the people of Israel, therefore you shall not bring this assembly into the

land that I have given them."
(Numbers 20:12 ESV)

In other words, Moses's punishment for this event was that he would not be allowed to enter the promised land. As Moses moved away from this moment, he held on to the hope that God would extend forgiveness and allow him to enter Canaan. How do we know that? Look at the following excerpts from the passage from Deuteronomy 3:

- Verse 23: "And I pleaded with the LORD . . ."
- Verse 24: "O LORD God, you have only begun to show your servant your greatness and your mighty hand . . ."
- Verse 25: "Please let me go . . ."

But Moses didn't encounter a sympathetic ear from the Lord. He deflected responsibility, which people tend to do when confronted with consequences related to their poor behavior. Based on the language used in this passage, this was a conversation of which God was growing weary:

- Verse 26: "But the LORD was angry with me because of you and would not listen to me. And the LORD said to me, 'Enough from you; do not speak to me of this matter again.'"

Try and imagine the emotion Moses must have been experiencing during this exchange. Anger. Disappointment. Resentment. Frustration. Proverbs tells us, "Hope deferred makes the heart sick, but a desire fulfilled is a tree of life." (Proverbs 13:12 ESV). Moses's desire was to lead Israel into Canaan . . . a hope that was deferred because the people refused to trust the Lord and invade Canaan (Numbers 14) and ultimately unfulfilled because of Moses's flippant behavior in the desert (Numbers 20). He must have felt sick.

As punishment for this incident in Numbers 20, God would not allow Moses to enter Canaan. *Transitioning to Joshua was not his punishment.* This is an important distinction. Transition itself is not a punishment!

Succession represents a shift, not an end. I am convinced that a retirement-based transition is not the last great thing a leader does, but the gateway to their greatest season of influence.

The tension Steve expressed at our lunch in 2007 came from his fear that retirement meant he would no longer be relevant. There is nothing further from the truth. But he needed to be filled with a dose of courage for the journey. Perhaps you need a dose of courage as well.

Moses's journey was difficult because he was dealing with the consequence of his own action. For others, the source of their unhealthy emotion springs from other areas. Here are four common unhealthy emotional expressions I observe in pastors and ministry leaders:

Fear: Not knowing what lies ahead causes many leaders to think they can simply ignore the topic of succession. One executive pastor shared with me that fifteen years earlier, the senior pastor clearly stated his desire to be proactive in planning his eventual transition. When it came time to begin planning, however, no one could bring the topic up. The bold declaration of years past meant nothing when it was time to act. His faith had withered into fear.

Disappointment: Some leaders feel a deep sense of discouragement as they approach retirement because they didn't achieve the same results as their friends and colleagues. This leads some to artificially extend their tenure, chasing one last initiative in a desperate attempt to feel significant.

Insecurity: Feelings of insecurity often become exposed as other leaders bring up the topic of succession. This unchecked emotion can compel a leader to question the loyalty of trusted, long-term friends and allies. One particular story breaks my heart to this day. The Senior Pastor and his family were close with one of the lay Elder's family. So close, they would vacation together annually. By the time I was called in to provide help, these two decades-old friends could not even speak to one another. The pastor's insecurity is ultimately what destroyed their friendship.

Sadness: Several of the pastors I have worked with express a deep sense of sorrow as they contemplate stepping away from a position that has provided a sense of significance and routine. They miss their office. They miss the meetings—even the ones they complained about attending. Even before the transition takes place, they anticipate missing the people with whom they serve. But most of all, they miss feeling needed.

If gone unchecked, these emotions have the potential to lead ministry leaders into patterns of behavior that contradict their character. This is confusing and frustrating for them, the leaders with whom they serve, and the people in their ministry.

You may remember a reference to Pastor Randy and his predecessor Bruce. Randy was kind enough to provide a candid peek into how emotion affected him and his staff.

> The elders had agreed, after much prayer, on an external search, rather than an internal candidate. When we informed

the team, they received the news soberly. A change of this magnitude hit them hard. Some worried about their future. One decided to accept a position as a solo pastor out west. Now understaffed, the workload and change created a lot of angst. As time wore on, I wrongly interpreted emotional comments of staff members as disrespectful. I wrestled with anger and sadness. In hindsight, I realize they felt frustrated (left out of decisions) and fearful (wondering what would happen).

Retirement-based transitions are critical seasons in which leaders must guard their hearts (Proverbs 4:23). Allowing your emotions to drive your words and behaviors carries a substantial consequence. Unbridled and unchecked emotions can destroy your reputation and damage relationships. James says a person's tongue can stain their entire body and set fire to their life (James 3:6).

Be mindful of your emotions. Don't allow them to drive you to actions and words you will regret.

What specific emotions do you currently have a hard time controlling? How could these emotions become harmful during your transition? Use the space below to record your thoughts.

Pisgah Forces the Leader to Consider the Needs of the People

Deuteronomy 3:23-28 and Numbers 27:12-23 are parallel passages that provide different insights into Moses's encounter with God at Pisgah. The Deuteronomy account shows us how emotionally charged the conversation was. Numbers illustrates how much Moses genuinely cared for the people.

> Moses spoke to the LORD, saying, "Let the LORD, the God of the spirits of all flesh, appoint a man over the congregation who shall go out before them and come in before them, who shall lead them out and bring them

in, that the congregation of the LORD may not be as sheep that have no shepherd." (Numbers 27:16–17 ESV)

This, from the same person who had this to say: "But the LORD was angry with me because of you and would not listen to me" (Deuteronomy 3:26 ESV). Moses genuinely loved the people, even though they drove him crazy at times. Every pastor I work with expresses the same tension. They love the people they serve . . . most of the time.

To truly appreciate the significance of what happened on Pisgah, let's take a quick trip through Moses's history by looking at two specific passages: Exodus 18 and Numbers 26. The former took place around four decades earlier. The events of Numbers 26 played out in the months preceding the events of Numbers 27.

Exodus 18 takes place just after Israel crossed the Red Sea:

- Exodus 18:1–7: Moses is reunited with his family.

- Exodus 18:8–13: Moses and his father-in-law Jethro celebrate God's deliverance of Israel.
- Exodus 18:14–18: Jethro asks Moses why he leads the people on his own.
- Exodus 18:19–23: Jethro recommends Moses appoint men to help judge the people.
- Exodus 18:24–26: Moses listens to Jethro's advice and establishes the following structure: Moses chose able men out of all Israel and made them heads over the people, chiefs of thousands, of hundreds, of fifties, and of tens. And they judged the people at all times. Any hard case they brought to Moses, but any small matter they decided themselves."

Now fast forward approximately forty years to Numbers 26, where God instructs Moses to take a census of the people. Verse 2 gives us the parameters for the census: ". . . [males] from twenty years old and upward, by their fathers' houses, all in Israel who are able to go to war." Verse 53 gives us the purpose of the census: "Among these the land shall be divided for inheritance according to the number of names."

Now we arrive at Numbers 27. By this time in Israel's journey, the organizational structure that Moses established in Exodus 18 had over thirty-five years to mature and develop. Israel had also just finished conducting the census that would be used to determine how the land would be allocated once they settled in Canaan. With these two big ideas in mind, we start into Numbers 27.

> Then drew near the daughters of Zelophehad the son of Hepher, son of Gilead, son of Machir, son of Manasseh, from the clans of Manasseh the son of Joseph. The names of the daughters were: Mahlah, Noah, Hoglah, Milcah, and Tirzah. (Numbers 27:1 ESV)

We first come across the daughters of Zelophehad listed as part of the census recorded in Numbers 26. This seems like a strange piece of information considering the count was explicitly designed to account for males aged twenty and older who were able to fight.

> And they stood before Moses and before Eleazar the priest and before the chiefs and all the congregation, at the entrance of the tent of meeting . . . (Numbers 27:2 ESV)

How did the daughters gain this level of access to the leaders of Israel? Given the structure outlined by Jethro in Exodus 18, the daughters' question would have first needed to work through the "chiefs of thousands, of hundreds, of fifties, and of tens." Evidently none of them had an answer to the daughters' question, so their issue finally ended up before Moses. In other words, they worked through the organizational structure initially established in Exodus 18.

So, what was their issue?

> Our father died in the wilderness . . . and he had no sons.

> Why should the name of our father be taken away from his clan because he had no son? Give to us a possession among our father's brothers. (Numbers 27:3–4 ESV)

According to Numbers 26, the land of Canaan would be distributed based on the census of males aged twenty and older. But the father of these women was dead, which meant they would have no land or source of provision once they entered into the new land. Theirs was a question of inheritance that carried significant personal consequence.

In verses 5-11 we are told that Moses took their request before the Lord. God granted the daughters of Zelophehad inheritance rights and established rules by which land was transferred.

Now we come to verses 12-23, where God instructs Moses to appoint Joshua as his successor.

Verses 12-15 tell us that God took Moses up the mountain to see Canaan. The Lord reminded Moses why he was not allowed to lead Israel into the promised land. Ouch!

Remember Moses's comments about the people in Deuteronomy 3:26, where he blamed them for his not being allowed to enter Canaan? Numbers 27 gives us an expanded picture of how that conversation played out.

> Let the LORD, the God of the spirits of all flesh, appoint a man over the congregation who shall go out before them and come in before them, who shall lead them out and bring them in, that the congregation of the LORD may not be as a sheep that have no shepherd. (Numbers 27:16 ESV)

On the heels of a question related to inheritance law and land rights, God brought Moses to Pisgah. When confronted with the reality of his own mortality, Moses asked the Lord a question. "Hey God, who is going to inherit my position . . . my leadership?"

What was his driving concern? "That the congregation of the LORD may not be as sheep that have no shepherd" (Numbers 27:17 ESV).

During the census, the daughters of Zelophehad became concerned about their fate, so they navigated their way through the structure and hierarchy, established over three decades earlier, with a question related to the possibility of their inheritance. They ended up face-to-face with Moses and the other leaders of the nation, the equivalent of the United States Supreme Court. Moses took their request to the Lord, from whom he received a response. On the heels of that conversation, God took Moses to Pisgah and let him know that he would soon be dead. In response, Moses asked God to appoint someone who would inherit his leadership. What a journey!

God used the circumstance of the census to force Moses to consider how a leadership void would impact the people. This was the moment Moses felt the weight of his departure. They would need a new "shepherd" to guide them into Canaan.

In preparing for Randy's retirement, the church leaders paused to consider the various things the people would need in order to navigate his transition. One of the things they did was create a five-year strategic plan, with at least half of that time extending beyond Randy's tenure. This was done so the people would see Randy's transition in the context of a broader movement toward where God was leading them. The clear pathway forward created an environment in which the people of the church knew where they would be going after Randy's transition.

What will it take to shepherd the people you lead through a season of transition? The various strategies used will look different from ministry to ministry. Here are a few questions to consider as you contemplate the needs of the people impacted by your eventual transition:

- Will they see your willingness to embrace your transition?
- Will they see your ability to manage, not hide, your emotions?
- Will they see a commitment to navigate a well-thought-out transition process?

- Will they see the willingness, humility, and courage to acknowledge current realities (the good, the bad, and the ugly)?
- Will they see genuine excitement about the future—both personally and for the ministry?

––––––––––––––––

Use the space provided to write a few specific things you feel your people will need.

Pisgah Forces the Leader to Consider the Successor

Joshua, as you are aware, would become Moses's successor. So, before we dig into the Numbers 27 and Deuteronomy 3 passages, let's use excerpts from Numbers 13 to review Joshua's resume.

> The LORD spoke to Moses, saying, "Send men to spy out the land of Canaan, which I am giving to the people of Israel. From each tribe of their fathers you shall send a man, every one a chief among them." (Numbers 13:1–2 ESV)

From the tribe of Ephraim, Hosea the son of Nun. (Numbers 13:8 ESV)

And Moses called Hosea the son of Nun, Joshua. (Numbers 13:16 ESV)

Then Joshua the son of Nun and Caleb the son of Jephunneh, who were among those who had spied out the land, tore their clothes and said to all the congregation of the people of Israel, "The land, which we passed through to spy it out, is an exceedingly good land. If the LORD delights in us, he will bring us into this land and give it to us, a land that flows with milk and honey. Only do not rebel against the LORD. And do not fear the people of the land, for they are bread for us. Their protection is removed from them, and the LORD is with us;

do not fear them." (Numbers 14:6–9 ESV)

Joshua was chosen to represent his tribe as one of twelve men selected to spy on Canaan. He was also a chief, which meant he was trusted to judge the affairs of the people (remember Jethro's recommendation from Exodus 18). He was respected within his tribe, and Moses knew him well enough to change his name.

We now come to our primary texts.

> So the Lord said to Moses, "Take Joshua the son of Nun, a man in whom is the Spirit, and lay your hand on him. Make him stand before Eleazar the priest and all the congregation, and you shall commission him in their sight. You shall invest him with some of your authority, that all the congregation of the people of Israel may obey. And he shall stand before Eleazar the priest, who shall in-

quire for him by the judgment of the Urim before the Lord. At his word they shall go out, and at his word they shall come in, both he and all the people of Israel with him, the whole congregation. (Numbers 27:18–21 ESV)

But charge Joshua, and encourage and strengthen him, for he shall go over at the head of this people, and he shall put them in possession of the land that you shall see. (Deuteronomy 3:28 ESV)

Here is a quick summary of the things God instructed Moses to do with Joshua at his initial installation:

- "Lay your hands on him" (Numbers 27:18)
- "Make him stand before Eleazar the priest and all the congregation" (Numbers 27:19)

- "You shall commission him in their sight" (Numbers 27:19)
- "You shall invest him with some of your authority" (Numbers 27:20)
- "Charge" (Deuteronomy 3:28)
- "Encourage" (Deuteronomy 3:28)
- "Strengthen" (Deuteronomy 3:28)

Why would God have Moses go through all of this effort? After all, Joshua was a known quantity. The current generation was aware of who he was. Wouldn't it be simple enough for Moses to announce he was promoting an internal successor and move on?

I believe the answer is no, for two primary reasons. First, this was the first leadership transition the nation of Israel would encounter. Moses was the person God had used to lead Israel out of bondage. He had spoken with God face-to-face. Moses was the only point man the nation had ever known, and he knew his absence would be felt.

Second, the people were fickle. It seemed as though any time they faced opposition, they would complain about leaving Egypt. There is no doubt that a leadership transition would be another excuse to complain and give rise to division and power struggles.

So God gave Moses instructions for how to transfer his leadership to Joshua, which, based on a careful study of Scripture, took place over several key moments. The first of these is recorded in our texts—Numbers 27 and Deuteronomy 3.

Like Moses, some retiring leaders know who their successor will be. Others do not. Regardless of your context, you can lend your influence to show the people what it looks like to follow someone else's lead. To not do so would be selfish, short-sighted, and a violation of our final principle: Pisgah forces the leader to consider their successor.

———————————————

What are two or three specific things you can do to prepare the way for your successor, whether you know them or not?

Here are the four principles we covered in Section 1:

Principle 1: Pisgah represents a shift, not an end.

Principle 2: The road to Pisgah is emotional.

Principle 3: Pisgah forces the leader to consider the people.

Principle 4: Pisgah forces the leader to consider the successor.

Section 2 puts skin and bones on these four principles. Pastors that have embraced Pisgah wrote the stories you are about to read. Where you may see Pisgah on the horizon, they see Pisgah in their past. May their words be a source of confrontation, challenge, and encouragement to your soul.

SECTION 2

Dr. Jeff Adams

Jeff Adams, PhD, spent a decade pastoring in Costa Rica, Nicaragua, and El Salvador before accepting the call to be the lead pastor of Graceway in Kansas City, Missouri, in 1984. During his thirty-three-year tenure at Graceway, Jeff developed a reputation for expository teaching, disciple-making, and leadership in global missions. Dr. Adams's global focus has taken him to over seventy countries while serving on boards and consulting with various agencies and organizations while leading Graceway's extensive missional engagement.

Formal planning for his succession process began in 2015 and concluded in 2017, passing leadership to Pastor Tim Dunn after a six-month overlap. Today, Jeff still continues a healthy relationship with Graceway, teaching a weekly Spanish Bible study, as well as other occasional teachings. He also is the board chair of Christar US and serves on Christar's international board. His primary focus, however, is equipping strategic leaders for maximum impact in a culturally complex world. He does this as a certified Paterson LifePlan Guide while mobilizing, training, and mentoring leaders in both the Spanish and English-speaking worlds.

Pisgah Represents a Shift, Not an End

I had been a pastor in four countries and two languages over the space of almost fifty years. By this time, I knew that the end of my pastoral ministry was fast approaching—I was tired. Will Heath was not only our succession consultant; he was a dear friend who had repeatedly emphasized the need to be certain I had been with Moses on Mt. Pisgah. Not only had I been on Mt. Pisgah; I had planted my flag there! I was ready to turn the reigns over to a younger, more energetic leader. I was NOT, however, ready to retire. My internal wiring simply does not allow for the thought of traditional retirement.

Observing several close friends move into "retirement" through a pastoral transition had been sobering for me. None of their stories had ended well. In almost every case, the transitioning pastor reneged on the decision or continued to express power behind the scenes. That taught me that once a leader visits Pisgah, there can be no turning back. I also knew that I could not stop being the person God created and gifted me to be. I was looking for more purpose and ministry, not less. But how that was supposed to look eluded me.

My pastoral life had revolved around expository Bible teaching, disciple-making (especially reproducing myself in younger leaders), and God's global mission to the forgotten peoples of the world. Withdrawing from what had driven me for half a century was unthinkable. I had offers in the academic world and executive roles in several substantial mission organizations. As tempting as those opportunities were at first glance, I was honest enough to know that administration and management were not my forte. To the contrary! They were what drained me and, in my mind, kept me back from more significant involvement in my areas of strength and passion.

I knew there had to be a way to continue meaningful ministry after my "retirement" from being a lead pastor. How to do that was still not clear. It was the next marker on the road to Pisgah that gave me clarity, but getting there was extremely painful and almost killed me.

The Road to Pisgah Is Emotional

I was in my late sixties as I moved through this process, and I can honestly say that I possessed a reasonably good self-awareness. I had never been a driven, controlling type of leader. No problem, right?

Wrong!

My emotions kicked me in the gut and took me completely by surprise. Precisely as we moved seriously into the years leading up to the actual transition, our executive pastor retired somewhat suddenly, and my bilingual executive assistant followed her husband as he accepted a pastorate in New England. Remember, I don't do well with the administration, management, and detail-oriented aspects of being a pastor. Knowing that we were moving irreversibly toward transition, the board and I recognized it would be folly to make such critical hires entering into the transition. It would be highly unfair to the new pastor, whoever he turned out to be, to be saddled with people in these key positions who were not of his choosing. In addition to my regular responsibilities as lead pastor and my considerable missional involvement outside the church, I was also functioning as the executive pastor and my own executive assistant. I was working eighty-hour weeks and becoming more miserable, frustrated, and exhausted by the day.

I knew I was in trouble. The board knew I was in trouble. Even Will could sense I was in trouble and recommended the board hire a life coach to work with me.

The idea repulsed me. I didn't have time now. Why would I want to spend an hour on the phone each week with someone who didn't know me? Feeling bad for appearing to be ungrateful, I apologized to Will. I just couldn't relate to the life coach idea, but I appreciated the thought. I told Will that I had a friend in California who had offered to take me through a LifePlan . . . whatever that is.

That was the moment my life shifted. "Wait," said Will, "is he a certified Paterson LifePlan facilitator?"

"Yeah, I think that's what he said."

Will looked me straight in the eyes and said with a forcefulness I had never known from him, "Do that!"

My wife and I were soon on a flight to San Diego. I wasn't sure what I was getting into, but I was desperate. I just wanted someone to tell me what to do. My emotions were going crazy!

The LifePlan process consists of two eight-hour days of over twenty exercises, involving discussions and Socratic questions designed to surface one's unique purpose and arrange every sphere of life around that purpose. I was sure it wouldn't work for me, but I was soon weeping as I clearly defined in a few short words my reason for existing on Planet Earth.

The key moment came when my facilitator friend said, "You're not entering a new season of life. You're being set free from the stuff you don't like, the stuff that drains you and, quite frankly, the stuff you're not good at, to be set free to do what you've been doing these past many years." The confusion melted away, as hope and enthusiasm flowed into the space left vacant.

There were still emotions left to haunt me. Cleaning out my office was overwhelming. But on a Sunday in August, I passed the baton to a wonderful young man I genuinely love and admire. I went to bed that night, wondering what would happen. Upon awakening the next morning, I made the incredible discovery that I was still the same person. I had the same personality, experience, and talents. I was still a pastor, just no longer THE pastor.

Life had not come to an end. It shifted.

Pisgah Forces the Leader to Consider the Needs of the People

Even during the worst moments of my emotional and exhausting pathway leading down the mountain from Pisgah, I knew that this was not just about me. This was about God's church, not mine. I had convinced myself that I could still relate, deliver the goods on

Sunday morning, and make a meaningful contribution. That was all true . . . to a degree. In my more lucid moments, I knew that, even though the congregation loved me, I was no longer truly qualified to lead them to the promised land. I promise that I had not been smacking any big rocks with a shepherd's staff. I had simply done what God asked me to do, and now it was time to turn it over to someone else to take it further down the road.

Previously, my concern for the people was mostly a smokescreen for my own fear of turning them loose. What would they do without me? Now that I had come down from Pisgah, I could begin to see clearly again. This was not about me. It was about shifting my influence. No longer would I find my fulfillment in proclaiming God's word to the masses; I would enter into the fullness of a ministry mentoring strategic leaders. The more my LifePlan unfolded before my eyes, the more excited I became about my future.

If I truly loved the people of my church, I would rejoice with them as God led us to precisely the right person to take us to new heights. I would still be part of them, as we all concluded that my personality and talents allowed me to stay as part of the team in a new and reduced capacity. That's not possible for everyone, but it felt very good to me.

Once we identified God's man for the position, I quickly saw that the promised land I had dreamed about would materialize into reality under his energetic and directive leadership. This was for the church, not me.

I'm still considered part of the pastoral team, even though I really don't do much. The church and new pastor have honored us so wonderfully! We feel loved and wanted. Wednesday nights when I'm in town, I still teach the Spanish Bible study. I enjoy regular lunches with the new guy, and he seems to genuinely welcome my mentorship. I continue to serve on both the domestic and international boards of a global mission agency that allows me to train, consult, and teach regularly. I even became certified as a Paterson LifePlan Guide, affording me a great instrument to continue my ministry of equipping strategic leaders in a culturally complex world. The more I focus on ministering to other leaders, the more I confirm that this whole process was never about me—it was about God caring for His church.

Pisgah Forces the Leader to Consider the Successor

Joshua had been around a long time, but God had to be very specific to Moses that he was his successor. Not only is Pisgah about the people; it's also about who is going to follow in the leader's footsteps. My legacy is not about what I accomplished, but what will happen after I'm gone. My success is inseparable from that of my successor.

Church leadership was convinced that the next lead pastor was not yet among us, nor was he found in our immediate circle of friends and sister churches. Will's insistence that we hire a search firm was perhaps the hardest part of the process. It smacked of internet dating to this old mind.

It did not take long to calm my fears. The search firm was spiritual, sensitive, and highly professional. We were all amazed that God had a man in mind that was the perfect fit, the answer to our prayer list, as we were to his. We discovered common ground in our past and complete compatibility in things relating to both orthodoxy and orthopraxy.

My immediate mission was clear. God was calling me to be his new best friend, and my wife, his wife's new best friend. I was to use my influence to be the bridge for him to the congregation. I was to withdraw all of the funds from my credibility bank and use them to pave his road to success.

Now I could focus on the symbolic and ceremonial passing of authority to him. I gave him my office, my library, and a New Testament that a couple from our church had invested their lives in translating for an indigenous people group in South America—beautiful symbolism of Graceway's commitment to God's Word and global mission.

My emotions would still emerge to engulf me at the strangest and most embarrassing moments, but I learned to be okay with that. How could turning over leadership after thirty-three years not be emotional? Pisgah is clearly a time of death for many things, but it is also a time of incredible rebirth, and for entering into the time of my greatest influence and satisfaction. I'm busier than ever, but without the stress and pressure of carrying the weight of leading the church. I'm the same person, but a far happier and more fulfilled version of myself.

Tim Celek

Tim Celek served as The Crossing's Lead and Founding Pastor for exactly 30 years. The Crossing began on September 11, 1988. Over those 30 years of Tim's leadership, The Crossing grew from a handful of people to over 2,500. Tim's passion, first and foremost, has been to reach, touch and speak to those who are saying no to God giving them an opportunity over time to say yes to Jesus. Over 40% of the people who attend The Crossing state that The Crossing is there first ever church of record.

The community surrounding The Crossing changed significantly over the course of Tim's leadership. However, as a result of the vision Tim had for the church to be a place for ALL people, regardless of their spiritual, ethnic, cultural, economic, or educational backgrounds, The Crossing was able to morph along with the change. Today, over 45% of those who attend are from different ethnic and cultural backgrounds (other than Caucasian).

In was in 2010 when Tim heard the word *succession* for the first time in the context of leadership and pastoral transition. In 2013, Tim intentionally and systematically led both himself, the Board of the church, the staff and the congregation through a 5-year journey of change in senior leadership. The official transfer of leadership took place in September of 2018 on the church's 30th anniversary. Tim continues in a reduced role on staff, supporting the vision of The Crossing and the next generation of leadership at the church in his new role as Founding Pastor.

The transition process has ignited in Tim a desire to "pay it forward." Tim is now spending larger portions of time coaching and consulting post-launch church planters as well as assisting churches to intentionally think through the all-important nature of a leadership transition on a local church.

Tim lives in Costa Mesa, with Sue, his wife of 40 years. They are parents and grandparents. Tim enjoys riding his Harley with Sue and spending time with his growing family.

Pisgah Represents a Shift, Not an End

Ever heard of the Baader-Meinhof phenomenon? I didn't think so! How about "frequency illusion"? Even if you aren't familiar with these specific words, I am pretty sure we've all experienced the sensation. Both of these terms describe the syndrome where the concept or thing you just found out about, or possibly desire, now seems to pop up everywhere. Think about the car you want to purchase and how you notice it around every corner and on every street you travel.

This phenomenon took me by surprise with the oddest of words. Frankly, it was a word I am almost convinced, even in this new context, I had never heard of previously. The concept had not really ever crossed my mind. Yet, once I noticed this word, the presence of articles and books addressing it, the numerous types of businesses that facilitated it, both secular and sacred, and the various paths and processes to take to accomplish the desired result were seemingly omnipresent.

The word is *succession*. Okay, I am not altogether ignorant. Sure, I was aware of the concept. It is often used to describe things that come one right after another. Still, I had not considered this word in terms of *me*.

However, here I was sitting in a mentoring group led by a pastor I respect, when all of a sudden, he mentioned that he had begun his process of succession. Little did I know how God would orchestrate the trajectory of my heart, mind, and life from that point in 2010. I was fifty-one years of age. Looking back, this was my "Pisgah" moment. Heading to the mentoring meeting, I didn't have any understanding of succession. Walking away from it, God had sparked something that absolutely altered the course of my life.

Almost immediately, and in the days, weeks, months, and years that followed, God dropped these nuggets of information and insight in supernatural ways. One of the absolute biggest was a series of videos produced and presented by Will Heath. I watched and rewatched every single one of them.

These videos allowed me to gain both a biblical and technical understanding of the journey I was about to embark on as I headed down Mt. Pisgah. One of the many vital learnings was that this probable transition would simply be *a shift, not an ending point*, for both the church and me. In those early days, and even now, I didn't see this as a step of *retirement*. Yet, almost to a person, those I would talk with (particularly in ministry) only saw it through the lens of this one word.

For example, after watching these videos, I frequently floated to various acquaintances, mentors, and friends in church leadership positions the idea of stepping down before sixty years of age and handing off the senior pastor role to a younger leader. The response was always the same: "That's great, it's neat you're thinking this way, but you are way too young to retire."

My response was always the same in turn. After so many interactions, it was almost rehearsed. "Who said anything about retirement? I am not retiring. I'm not sure I believe in retiring. I am simply doing something that is best for the church we planted in the fall of 1988. And it's paramount that I do it now while I still have tons in the tank, not when either the church or I am on our last leg."

I'd say, "Think how awesome it is that I get to be a part of the new person's selection. I get to build into and mentor the new leader. My wife and I can come alongside the new couple, so they have folks who encourage them. We wanted that when we launched the church but didn't have that support. Plus, this is how God wants it."

I'd say, "Moses built into Joshua, and the people of God were able to enter the promised land. I want that for The Crossing Church. Elijah built into Elisha. Elisha even asked for a double portion of God's Spirit that was on Elijah. What new leader wouldn't desire a 'doubling' of all God did through their life?

"This is just succession, a passing of the baton for a new generation. It's not an ending point; it's a sweet new beginning. The best part is I get to lend my influence on the entire process. It's like the best of all worlds."

The Road to Pisgah Is Emotional

Having said all of the above, this journey, while positive and best for the church and me, is laden with more than a few emotional highs and lows.

Some of my highest highs were at my wedding to my bride, with whom I'm now going on forty years of marriage, or the great joy surrounding the birth of my two daughters, then years later the incredible celebrations at their beautiful weddings! And through the years there have been lows as well, like conducting the memorial services for congregants, friends, or family members.

Believe me, having experienced this journey of succession, there is a great deal of truth in that the emotions, while in the trenches of it all, feel very much like presiding over the joy surrounding sweet wedding festivities. On the other hand, honestly, it also felt like I was assisting in the management of a grieving group at a memorial. Let me see if I can make sense of some of these thoughts.

The board and I watched Will's online succession coaching videos and read other succession-related books together. For the most part, this was all done four years before the actual handoff.

During this stretch, I was lulled into a false sense, both for myself and for our church, that this journey, personally and corporately, would be an emotionally easy one.

When you're four years out, the dialogue stays at an intellectual level. These interchanges are a necessary component of the wild ride of change any church or organization embarks on as the result of succession. Yet, it wasn't until I set the actual date for my departure that lots of emotions rose to the surface.

I felt the best timing for the transition would be the church's thirtieth anniversary. My wife Sue and I had the privilege of giving birth to this new church in Costa Mesa, California, in 1988. I sensed God's prompting that the delight of the delivery could be relived during this momentous thirty-year marker.

However, even though I found incredible energy recasting the vision of The Crossing during the year-long communication and handoff journey that culminated on our thirtieth anniversary, the entire course of events was bittersweet.

We held group communication after group communication. During each, I lifted up my successor. It was not hard to do, as I felt God's confirmation in his new leadership. With each successive communication, however, I became more and more aware that I would not be a critical cog on the next leg of the journey. I knew we had God's man for this new season, yet I would often walk away and think quietly to myself, "I still have a *lot* left in the tank. God, really?"

Full disclosure: even though I was the one who initiated the plan for succession, I knew I didn't want to be "that pastor" who overstayed. But let me tell you, after multiple conversations, following group presentations, or during board discussions, I would have a ton of people saying these sorts of words, often with tears in their eyes:

"But you are so young! You have so much energy! You are at the top of your game! You are the reason I come to this church! My family and I, or my wife and I, or our kids, we/they now have Jesus because of your pastoral leadership. We love you. Tim, I mean, I respect you greatly, but are you sure you're making the right decision?"

I would be less than honest to say that during and after every one of those interactions, there wasn't a *big* part of my ego that wanted to say, "You're right! This is insane. Okay, I'll stay."

Yet, I wouldn't allow those thoughts to linger. I knew of pastors who had let those sentiments seep into the well of their soul. As a result, they did an about-face. The church's landscape is littered with the fallout of pastors who reneged on their promised departure. I don't believe any of them intended it to be so; emotion just got the best of them.

As for me, as called as I had felt to start The Crossing, I felt just as called to hand it off. The decision to launch it wasn't about me; the decision to leave it in new hands wasn't about me, either. I kept resting on the reality that this decision was what was best for the church.

Just know, the decision is the right decision, yet God made us fully human. So, the choice of transition IS emotional. Don't let emotions muddy the reality that what you are doing is the right thing to do!

Pisgah Forces the Leader to Consider the Needs of the People

I will say, since at its core the decision to transition was not about the pastor, but rather what is best for the church, it is an entirely clarifying one for a strategically-oriented leader. From the launch of The Crossing Church, I have sought to keep our church on mission. Any leader knows that mission drift, while not desired, can seem to happen over time.

Once the date was set for an official hand-off, it became crystal clear that moving forward, everything had to be directed toward what would provide the best overall environment for a successful season of change for the church and for the new leader.

So, my missional North Star was now to shepherd our board, our staff, our leaders and volunteers, our givers, our congregation, and the new leader through this journey of succession.

First, it meant guiding our board to answer the question, "Who would the new leader best be?" After many discussions based on what we watched, read, and prayed through, we decided the new leader would be from outside our church, yet would have the same basic "DNA" of our church. For us, this meant the mission would not change, yet the methods surrounding it might possibly be altered to more effectively accomplish the mission in this generation.

Second, we decided that we would enter into a season of *intentional overlap* for two years. This meant we were looking for a leader who desired to be mentored/coached during this season of successive and deliberate transfer of the various leadership roles and responsibilities.

Third, I knew both intuitively and from reality that, being the church's founder, much of its organizational dysfunction resulted from the weaknesses of my leadership. Therefore, now was the best time to uncover as much as possible—all the corporate confusion and systemic stupidity—and begin to bring organizational clarity and health to The Crossing.

Fourth, we would only move forward on organizational clarity once the new leader was found. In my heart, I felt the new leader needed to be present while various consultants assisted us in "peeking" under the covers as we looked at everything from strategic planning, staffing, structure, governance, finances, and ministry programming.

I found that having clarity around the decision to leave freed me up to enter into the many necessary discussions and dialogues with a fully positive disposition. Truthfully, many of these conversations were difficult; they showed me where I made leadership mistakes over the years. Yet, because I wanted ultimate success for our church and for our new leader, I was able to fully embrace whatever was necessary to position both him and our church for a new season of God's supernatural work that would last well into the future.

Pisgah Forces the Leader to Consider the Successor

I know many churches where the departing leader does not get the opportunity to weigh in on or take part in the new leader's life.

There is a big part of me that grieves for both the church and the transitioning leader.

As a result of my research and reading, I know that many "founders" or long-tenured senior pastors of churches have gummed up the works in multiple ways, such that it makes life for the new leader problematic and unpleasant. Again, it makes me sad to see such selfishness.

I mean, who among us does not want to have someone in our corner? Who among us doesn't want to have a mentor or a coach who desires to see us soar beyond our wildest imaginations?

As the departing leader, I decided, in advance, to invest time weekly into the new leader during the two-year run up to the handoff. I also decided to do this for two years after the transition, for coaching, mentoring, or simply listening.

Also, I felt it was important that my wife and I spend significant intentional, relational time with the new leader, his spouse, and their family. My wife would engage personally and regularly with his spouse, just the two of them. As a result, our relationship continues to this very day. As with my own kids, my deepest desire is only for their best.

I committed that publicly and privately, I would position the new leader in a positive light. As a result, I cannot begin to tell you the number of times board members, paid staff, or congregants say, "It's so neat to watch how much you are honoring him," or, "You two really get along!" or, "It's fun to see the endearing ways you tease one another."

Again, ready your emotions and ego, especially if you are involved in the process like I was! People will brag on the new pastor in front of you. People will say, "The change is refreshing." Or a staff member will state, "It's good that we finally get to collaborate and weigh in on things like never before."

Learn to smile and say with sincerity and humility, "Thank you for the input. I, too, am excited for our church and for his leadership."

It is with outright conviction that I am excited for The Crossing Church. It is a great church. God has used its people and its leaders throughout all these years to reach and grow up people very far from God. I am also thrilled about our new leader and how God is using him. To think God has allowed me the privilege and opportunity to be a part of it all is truly amazing.

Randy Scheil

Randy grew up in NW Iowa and came to know Jesus as a child in Vacation Bible School. He attended the University of Iowa where he was discipled by the Navigators. While leading Bible studies for students, he felt God's call to full time ministry.

While attending Dallas Theological Seminary, he joined the staff of Garland Bible Fellowship. Ordained in 1982, he served there until 1984. After working as youth pastor in South Dakota and solo pastor in NW Iowa, Randy came to Stonebridge Church in Cedar Rapids, Iowa, in 1992. The church, originally Cedar Hills Evangelical Free, changed their name to Stonebridge when the congregation relocated in 2008. Randy served for 27 years and "semi-retired" in August 2019.

Randy initiated discussions about transition with his elders in 2014. In September 2017, he and his board invited Will Heath for a succession consultation. The elders began communicating a transition plan to the congregation in February 2018. A search committee was launched in May 2018. In February 2019, the congregation called a new Lead Pastor.

Though Randy officially retired from Stonebridge in August 2019, he was redeployed in September with The Charles Simeon Trust as Associate Director of International Workshops. Simeon Trust equips pastors and ministry leaders to make progress in their reading, study and teaching of the Scriptures. Randy continues to work from Cedar Rapids, Iowa, where he lives with his wife, Cindy. His four children, their spouses and eight grandchildren live nearby.

Pisgah Represents a Shift, Not an End

As 2017 began, I was in my twenty-fifth year as lead pastor at Stonebridge, and our church was close to paying off the mortgage on our new building. We were primed to reach our community in greater ways than ever before. I was excited as I prayerfully drew a conceptual vision for a five-year plan of expansion. Staff and elders seemed receptive. At age sixty-four and blessed with good health, I believed I had the strength and vigor to tackle this new initiative.

Proverbs 16:9 says, "The heart of man plans his way, but the LORD establishes his steps." Shortly after unrolling the plan, my father passed away unexpectedly. As executor, I not only experienced sorrow, but I was responsible for dispensing of his home and possessions, which was challenging since he lived four hours away. By God's grace, much work was completed by the end of the summer. Then, in August, our worship pastor announced he was leaving to serve with a mission organization. The five-year plan assumed strong worship leadership. Grappling with these changes caused me to reevaluate. Was I the one to plunge into a search process for a new worship leader? Or did it make more sense to begin planning for my transition and leave this vital staff hire to a new lead pastor?

During this time, a friend recommended we consider working with Will as our consultant. He invested two days of counseling our elders on a reasonable plan for transition. When Will asked me for a timeline, I referred to the five-year plan in which I expressed a desire to be part-time by July 2019. I was convinced it would be good for our church to have a younger lead pastor. It would also free me to mentor pastors locally and internationally. Although I loved being the lead pastor, I was excited about a new season of opportunity.

My predecessor, Bruce, gave me a wonderful model for being "redeployed." He retired from our church a few months before I was called as pastor. He and his wife Eleanore met with us on our candidate weekend. He asked if we would mind if they stayed in our community and in the church. They planned to attend another church for several months, giving me time to establish my leadership role. Then they wanted to return as active members. I admit I was uncertain about this since I had heard stories of pastors who stayed but continued to control ministry in the background. Reluctantly, we agreed to give it a try.

After months of getting to know Bruce and Eleanore, we invited them to return to our fellowship. They graciously became our cheerleaders, advocates, friends, and ministry supporters. My children learned to play the piano sitting next to Eleanore! We hoped we could follow their example someday for the pastor and family who would succeed us.

The Road to Pisgah Is Emotional

When Will described the emotions Moses felt on Pisgah I wrongly believed I wouldn't have them. My overconfidence came because our elders designed a transition that seemed logical, reasonable, and effective. After reviewing our mission, values, and ministry strategies with Will, we agreed on an "Overlap" approach, rather than a "Stop and Go" or "Intentional Interim" strategy. The elders wanted me to remain for a time to help onboard our new lead pastor. After that, I would leave for a time and then come back, as my predecessor had done. We drew a timeline and designed a communication plan for the staff and congregation. It seemed seamless to me.

I was in for some surprises. First, I under-estimated the impact on our staff. The elders had agreed, after much prayer, on an external search, rather than an internal candidate. When we informed the team, they received the news soberly. A change of this magnitude hit them hard. Some worried about their future. One decided to accept a position as a solo pastor out west. Now understaffed, the workload and change created a lot of angst. As time wore on, I wrongly interpreted emotional comments of staff members as disrespectful. I wrestled with anger and sadness. In hindsight, I realize they felt frustrated (left out of decisions) and fearful (wondering what would happen).

I was also unprepared for the emotions of our congregation. We communicated our plan in February 2018. Before long, people approached me. One asked, "Do you really *want* to retire?" A lady said, "You are too young to retire. Won't you reconsider?" I wondered, is she right? Did I quit too soon? A man put his hand on my shoulder. "Randy, I want you to know how much you mean to my family and me. We will miss you." He recalled how I had walked with him and his wife through tough times. When I saw the tears in his eyes, I was moved.

I felt like a "lame duck," though I know people didn't intend to treat me as one. When the search committee interviewed candidates, they were excited. Their comments became a gut check for me, even though I was excited too. Elders no longer needed my input on certain issues. Though I rejoiced to see them take responsibility for the process, I felt sad when decisions were made without consulting me or telling me why they were made.

As a pastor, I've been clear about my role in teaching, building leaders, and pastoral care. I had not considered what I would do following my transition. I began to worry about the future. I felt sad as I packed up my office, sorting books to give away. Every tossed file held past memories. Then my wife reminded me that I was a Christian before I was a pastor! My identity is in Christ, just as it was in the eight years I worked in the medical field as a layman before becoming a pastor. God would not abandon me.

Pisgah Forces the Leader to Consider the Needs of the People

I was inspired by Will's thoughts on Moses's trip to Pisgah's peak. Moses wanted to lead the Israelites into the promised land (Deuteronomy 3:23–28). This was not the Lord's plan. As Moses accepted God's will, he saw the need for strong leadership for the good of the people. But what *kind* of leader was needed? Would this person be committed to the continuity of the vision? Would he be willing to courageously take on the demands of the conquest? God chose Joshua, whom Moses had mentored through the years.

Before my sabbatical five years ago, I told the elders I was thinking about succession. I knew my transition was inevitable at some point. I said to the board, "I'm not ready to retire, but I know it is in the future. I'm not afraid to discuss it with you. I want to use part of my sabbatical to learn about healthy transitions and interview pastors who have done it well. Christ is the Head of our church, not me, and I long for this congregation to thrive after I'm gone." The elders appreciated my proactive stance. I learned so much from the pastors I interviewed—both outgoing and incoming leaders. This led to many fruitful conversations with our elders.

In a few short years, the season for transition arrived. Yet I was concerned about stalling the momentum of ministry. A church can be so focused on retirement and a search for a new pastor that outreach and discipleship become secondary. I loved the church too much for this to happen! When Will suggested the staff and elders develop a five-year vision, I immediately recommended it. We invested two full days in January 2018. The results were amazing. After researching our community, we learned that our area, the 52404 zip code, is the most under-resourced part of our city. A growing number of immigrants and single parents have unmet daily needs. Our vision plan was designed to meet the physical and spiritual needs of 404 families while also developing leaders to serve them.

Since our ministry year is August 1 to July 31, we wanted to jump-start the vision in April after four months of prayer. We set a goal for 10,000 prayer connections and asked our congregation to self-report on prayer activities in LIFE Groups, prayer walks, the National Day of Prayer, and other initiatives. God enabled us to exceed our goal, with over 15,000 prayer connections! When August 1 arrived, opportunities were waiting. We built and supplied a food and clothing pantry in a nearby elementary school, read to young children starting to learn English, and taught women cooking and budgeting skills in a substance rehabilitation center.

God blessed our 404 initiative with fruit and enabled us to focus on something other than transition. Praying together created a more profound sense of unity. Serving together to meet our community's needs caused our congregation to grow spiritually as we wrestled with how God was calling us to serve and live on-mission in our daily lives. This was a vision that would live beyond my tenure. It also gave clarity for the kind of leader we would be looking for in a new lead pastor.

Pisgah Forces the Leader to Consider the Successor

Moses mentored Joshua before he knew he would be his successor. Joshua was tested and had proved himself for years. Numbers 27:15–17 provides a list of his qualifications:

- He was Moses's assistant for years (Exodus 33:11).
- He and Caleb were courageous spies (Numbers 13–14).
- He knew the people well and was possessed of the Spirit (Numbers 27:18).
- God gave him wisdom he would need for the role of leadership (Numbers 27:21).

In our case, however, our leaders were convinced we should look for an external candidate. I was relieved when our elders and congregation voted to form a search committee and hire a search firm. From my own research, I knew the most significant change for a congregation, even greater than relocating, is transitioning from a long-tenured leader to an incoming lead pastor. I also knew that the most important aspect of an effective transition, next to a candidate affirming the church's mission, vision, and values, was friendship and mutual respect between the outgoing and the incoming pastor. I was prayerfully optimistic that God would provide what our congregation needed.

The search firm reviewed over a hundred resumes and interviewed candidates with the needs of Stonebridge in mind. In God's providence, we found a great fit in a man who, only one or two weeks before, had decided with his wife to be open to God's leading for a new ministry! Though I've known him for several years, in the months since we called him to be our lead pastor, I have grown in my respect and appreciation for him and his family. My primary goal is to help him take the leadership role and be effective. We worked together on several goals during our overlap period. My wife and I wanted to do all we could to welcome and support his family. I want to be to him what my predecessor was to me almost thirty years ago.

It is a "bittersweet" time: *bitter* because I love being a shepherd at this church—it was hard preaching my last sermon—yet *sweet* in that God provided a great leader to step into my role. I am convinced that the best years of Stonebridge are ahead of us! The Lord has calmed my fears about the future. I've received invitations for ministry opportunities that involve equipping pastors internationally to study and teach the Bible, serving as a pastoral and church health coach for our EFCA district in Eastern Iowa, and preaching regularly at a state prison nearby. Before the transition, Cindy and I would go on "retirement dates." I wanted to hear her thoughts about my transition. After all, she was transitioning too. Together we felt the loss of many things. But we also looked forward with the anticipation of being redeployed in the service of King Jesus.

James Robinson

James Robinson began his service to the local church while a freshman at Oklahoma Baptist University, beginning what would become fourteen years in youth ministry and thirty-six years as lead pastor. He retired as senior-pastor of First Baptist Church, Durant, Oklahoma, in 2018 after a tenure of nearly nineteen years.

Upon retirement, James and his wife, Judy, joined the staff of Double Honor Ministries as Pastor to Pastors. Double Honor Ministries serves clergy, pastors, ministry leaders and spouses by providing free respite retreats in a safe, refreshing, encouraging and supportive environment.

James and Judy live in Durant, Oklahoma, and are blessed with their adult children and eight grandchildren.

Pisgah Represents a Shift, Not an End

For years I had watched the difference between pastors who retired "from" their church while others retired "to" another ministry. I was determined to do the latter. I knew there would be a time to move from one way of serving Christ and his kingdom to another. But after fifty years of serving a local church, I wanted to know that there was a new adventure waiting for Judy and me.

The end of some things would not make me sad, like committee meetings, dealing with conflict, and staying on top of facility issues. However, the end of others would: preaching through an entire book of the Bible to my flock week in and week out and the study time that came with that; standing in the baptistry with children, youths, and adults who were making their public announcement of following Jesus; bonding with a team of ministers who were so different but just as committed as I am. These and other things would be difficult to stop doing, but the prospect of a new adventure looming—one that I felt just as called to do—made this transition not only doable but exciting.

As is always the case, the Lord has the supply before we have the need. For three years before my "shift," my wife and I had volunteered for a ministry called Double Honor. They minister to the pastor as a person, not a professional, by facilitating couples' retreats. As I retired, my concern for those serving as ministry leaders in the church was profound. I assumed my new role would be to encourage them as I preached in different pulpits. However, God had much broader and more significant plans. The ministry leaders of Double Honor asked if Judy and I would consider joining them on staff as "pastor to pastors." It opened up a door precisely where our passion was.

The Road to Pisgah Is Emotional
Wow!

Before transitioning, I really didn't know what those emotions would be for me. I was so caught up in leading my church into something they had never done—"planned succession"—that I really didn't think much about my emotions. Even on my last Sunday, the worship service was overwhelmingly excellent. Judy and I felt as though the people genuinely appreciated us. The first month of retirement felt like a month-long vacation. Something I was more than ready for.

But then came the second and third months.

So much of my life was driven by the rhythms of what happened on Sundays and Wednesdays. I wasn't sure what else to do. About two months after my retirement, I went back to the church to do a funeral. As I walked up to the church building, it hit me that I no longer had an office "hideout." I was the visiting preacher at the church I had pastored for almost nineteen years.

Judy was a real godsend for me during these months. The greatest gift she gave me for retirement was a home office. Judy would brush it off by saying my books didn't need to be stacked up in the bedroom. But she knew I needed this long before I did. She gave me a place that has become an unexpected joy. I am still in the process of "processing" my emotions. I have learned the importance of sharing them with some people I trust.

Pisgah Forces the Leader to Consider the Needs of the People

One of my predecessors had abruptly retired from the church after fifteen years of very fruitful ministry. The announcement of his retirement came on a Sunday night at the end of the service. He instructed the minister of music to lead the congregation in singing while he and his wife left the building. He would later tell me he was burned out and simply couldn't go on.

Even though another pastor had immediately succeeded him, he had become an "unintentional interim." I arrived about four years later, and the congregation was still somewhat in shock.

I did not want the church to have the same experience with me as they had with him. Learning from that story, I knew a planned succession would be something very new in this church, but I genuinely believed it would be the best way to prepare them for the future. I started talking "transition" publicly about a year before it happened. Initially, they didn't know how to talk about the future with the pastor still there.

However, when they saw my comfort with the idea, they began to warm to it, and many would thank me over the next year for leading them into this.

Taking a proactive posture in planning my succession helped the church avoid another "unintentional interim" situation.

The church rediscovered who they were. They had a new sense of clarity about the things they did well and their unique position for kingdom work.

However, if I am being candid, it is a stretch to say that my initial motivation was the well-being of the church. I was more concerned about the well-being of my eventual successor. After the transition of a long-tenured pastor, there can be panic, overreactions, and what might look like anarchy. What I so desired was a planned succession, a time to pause, reflect, and reaffirm the church's unique place in Christ's kingdom. But some of this reflection and reaffirmation was going to come *before* I left. I wasn't trying to control the process, but knew I needed to be involved with it. That summer, we hosted a series of "town hall" type meetings where people were encouraged to express their thoughts openly, not in secret whispers in the parking lot.

I was there, in a sense, giving them permission to speak candidly. Some, to be sure, didn't need permission. But others, who were very supportive of me, knew that changes needed to be made. I wanted them to be a part of the discussion. I wanted them to know it was ok to talk about these things in front of me. In many ways, it proved helpful. The transition would not be just a time to react but a time to reaffirm our mission and retool (if necessary) the way we carried out that mission. It reminded me of pruning. Painful? Indeed! But if done carefully, skillfully and with growth in mind, pruning always results in more fruit.

Pisgah Forces the Leader to Consider the Successor

I have been the successor!

I've followed the man who was more of a businessman than a pastor.

I've followed the man whose wife earned $30,000 a month as an executive of a worldwide company.

I've followed the man who had a fruitful, almost legendary ministry, and left "way too early."

I've stepped into situations with staff problems that should have been handled by the church *before* I got there.

I know what it means to follow long-tenured pastors who were loved and supported. But I also know what it's like to follow pastors who overstayed their welcome. I've felt the pressure to "figure it out" when the people didn't know how to move forward.

Over time, I have developed a heart for the "next guy." I wanted my successor, the next new guy at First Baptist, to start well. This meant I needed to allow certain things to happen under my watch. There were areas of pressure I needed to bear so he and his family would not have to. Most people in the church were focused on how the transition would impact them. Judy and I were more concerned about my successor's family . . . that they would be able to start well and establish a home.

Cal Rychener

Cal Rychener is the founding and senior pastor of Northwood's Church in Peoria, Illinois. From its inception in 1990 to its present day ministry 30 years later, Northwoods has been blessed to see God move in powerful ways to bring thousands of people to faith in Jesus Christ. Recently, through a fresh vision for church planting, Northwoods has partnered with the *Surge Project* and hopes to plant 3,000 churches globally, and 20 churches regionally by 2030. Already, the Lord's blessing has been evident as over 500 churches have been planted globally, a ministry school for church planters has been developed and the first regional church was launched in the fall of 2020.

In addition to his love for the local church, Cal has two other great passions. First and foremost is his wife Susan and their children Kathryn & Andy Rogers, Michaela & Jonathan Rychener, Victoria & Kody Pinson, and Nathan – plus 9 grandchildren and counting. Running a distant second is his love for the Green Bay Packers, for whom he has been a guest chaplain. Cal is also the author of two books, *Living at a Higher Level of Faith* and *God Can*.

Pisgah Represents a Shift, Not an End

As I write my story today, it differs a bit in perspective from those who have already transitioned, in that I'm still in the process of defining key elements of my transition and will be walking through it within the next few years. But make no mistake, successfully scaling Mt. Pisgah is the next leg of my leadership journey. So, I hope my unfolding story may be an encouragement to those of you who, like me, can see Pisgah rapidly approaching.

I knew going into our annual elders' retreat in September of 2018 that this one would be a little different from our past retreats. One of the topics for discussion was going to be my transition plan. We had engaged Will Heath to lead us through this discussion, and I had prepared myself as prayerfully as I could to be open and pliable to whatever I sensed God saying. Understand: my relationship with the elders was good; there was no desire on anyone's part to see me leave; I wasn't being forced out, and the elders were comfortable with me selecting a future date of my own choosing. Until that time, I had reasoned to myself, "Let's see, I planted the church in 1990. If I stayed until 2030, that would be a forty-year run (and that's as close to being like Moses as you can get). However, I'd be seventy-one at that point, and I'm pretty sure I don't want to run as hard as I've been running until I'm seventy-one. How about if I go until I'm sixty-six-years old? That would be 2025; I would have been leading Northwoods for thirty-five years, and that would give me another seven years to lead." So, going into the retreat, I was fully prepared to inform the elders that I would be ready to transition in 2025. Little did I know that Pisgah was even closer than that!

Of course, I had been feeling some gentle nudges and quiet whispers in my soul for some time whenever I would consider the fact that I was now somewhere in the fourth quarter of my leadership journey. For the past year or two, I had sensed an undeniable shift in my heart with regard to my passion for leading the church. But I would always push it down and tell myself, "Just keep going; after all, what are you going to do if not this?" That was the haunting question. For the past forty-one years of my life I had awakened each morning to the exciting journey of either preparing to lead (seven years) or actually leading (thirty-four years) a local church. The local church was my life; it had been the source of my highest highs and my lowest lows. Leading and growing a thriving, God-honoring, dynamic church had occupied my every waking moment since I had graduated from high school in 1977. What would my life be like apart from leading a local church?

As Will began unfolding Pisgah's dynamics, these disquieting questions and the gentle voice of the Holy Spirit came washing over my soul. "Cal, it's time to cast your faith forward and your fears behind you, as you have always done at major transition points in your life. I have never failed you! As I opened doors then, so I will open doors in the days ahead. I have not equipped you, anointed you, gifted you, given you all the leadership experiences, and shown you my mighty works, just to put you on a shelf for the rest of your life. Trust me as you face this transition; it is a shift, not an end! But today, I want you to begin moving toward transition." I knew in that one defining moment at our retreat that my transition was no further than three years away.

The Road to Pisgah Is Emotional

As I became aware that I was already at Pisgah, deep sobs began to well up in my soul. At the same time, I was trying hard just to reason myself out of this moment. "Maybe you're just tired and need some down time? And what is Susan (my wife) going to say if you go home and tell her that our transition date has been moved up to 2022?" I had tried to broach this subject with her several times before and it had usually ended up in an argument. Always, it seemed, we were on different pages. But over time, I realized that I needed to consider what my transition might mean for Susan, as her life had been equally invested in the local church our entire married lives. So much of her joy had been drawn from pouring into the lives of the kids in our children's ministry. What would she do if she wasn't teaching children each weekend? And if my future contained a lot of travel, what ministry would she have if she merely traveled with me?

Thankfully, our elders gifted us with an eight-week sabbatical (which we enjoyed during the months of February and March of 2019). This afforded us the time to get away, enjoy one another, talk, prayerfully reflect on issues related to transition, and make the wonderful discovery again. Our greatest joy is simply being a son and daughter of the King. That is who we were before we were ever called to lead a church, and that is who we are now. It was good to get clarity around the identity issue again: that though our roles and positions in the kingdom would inevitably change, our fundamental identities as redeemed, loved, and chosen children of the King never would.

Of course, as I've come to grips with the fact that I am not that far away from transitioning out of my senior pastor role, I find that tears are never far from the surface. Nostalgic memories sweep over my heart, and deep gratitude floods my soul for what I have been privileged to experience.

Emotion wells up at the awareness of how fast time has gone. How can it be that just yesterday, it seems, I was sitting in my Bible college classes dreaming about what ministry would be like, and here I am already facing transition?

Tears of joy arise as I remember awesome answers to prayer, miracles of provision, thousands of lives changed, and the thrill of leading a growing, dynamic church. Nothing was better than leading a church in those "up and to the right" seasons.

And of course, I have deep feelings concerning moments where I wish I'd done better; moments where I wish I'd led with a little more patience and love; feelings for staff members who left wounded. Today I want them to know how loved and appreciated they were, and are. I often wonder if Moses ever felt the sting of regret for having struck the rock.

I still feel deeply for some who, for whatever reason, couldn't make the journey with me. There are people whom I loved and ministered to but still ended up leaving disgruntled or dissatisfied. Then there are those who opposed my leadership. It makes me wonder if Moses felt the sting of rejection from Korah and others who rejected his leadership.

Finally, I grieve at the awareness that I will climb Pisgah with some of my dreams and longings unfulfilled. I think of what it was like for Moses, on top of Nebo, to look over into the promised land for which he had labored forty years, but which he would never experience. His leadership journey would end with some of his greatest hopes and dreams unfulfilled, and so will mine.

Pisgah Forces the Leader to Consider the Needs of the People

As I left the retreat that week, I was wrestling with the questions, "Is transitioning in three years too soon? Did I make that decision in the emotion of the moment? Am I going to be where I need to be financially in three years? Do I really want to leave another four or five years of salary on the table?" All of these thoughts rattling around in my brain would fall silent when I considered the one question that seemed to trump them all: what does our church most need in a leader for this next season of ministry, and am I the one to give that to them?

I was unprepared for how startlingly clearly the answer to that question had come into focus for me at the retreat. As Will was leading one of our sessions, he made a statement that brought penetrating insight into some feelings in my heart for which I couldn't find the words. He said something to the effect of, "Cal, you can no longer exegete and speak to today's culture like you used to because that demands a younger voice that is now a part of that culture." It reminded me of the passage in Acts 13:36 that says, "David served God's purpose in his own generation."

Increasingly I had been feeling a bit out of touch with this new, younger generation. Where they longed for collaborative leadership, I was more comfortable with visionary leadership. Where they were whizzes with modern-day technology, I struggled to learn and adapt. Where they were more comfortable with dialogue about today's issues, I was more comfortable with directives. It's a new day, and I've come to grips with the fact that our church needs new leadership to meet the needs of a new day. It's time for a new leader to serve God's purposes in this "now" generation.

Finally, the clincher for me was that I could not even imagine running hard for another seven years, whereas in years past I couldn't wait to climb the next hill, cast the next vision, slay the next giant, or go to the next level. I had to be honest that something inside me had shifted. I increasingly found myself thinking, "I don't enjoy the daily grind like I used to. There are some mountains that, were I asked to climb them today would make me almost sick." Leading yet another capital campaign is one such mountain. And whereas in years past I couldn't imagine myself not leading a church, I now found myself thinking, "I'm not sure I want to lead this anymore." All of these were signals to me that instead of hanging around for the next paycheck, it was time to consider our people's needs for a godly, energetic leader who was ready to tackle the issues of our day and take new ground.

Pisgah Forces the Leader to Consider the Successor

All of this has culminated in me asking, "So what does our church need for the future?" Surprisingly, considering that question has been incredibly liberating for me. I'm realizing today that there are some roles in the broader church that only older, seasoned leaders can play. When I consider those roles, my excitement level rises. I want to play the role of father, mentor, coach, and advisor to younger leaders. I want to be that older leader that a younger Joshua can lean on for wisdom, encouragement, and prayer. And having settled the issue of transition in my own heart, I find myself asking the question more and more, "Who are the younger leaders that I can pour into? How can I lift them up, encourage them, and walk alongside them?" My focus has shifted. It's kind of nice to be asking for the first time in my life, "How can I help that young leader become all he or she can be for the kingdom of God?" instead of asking, "How can I become all I can be for the kingdom of God?" Maybe that first question is the one I was supposed to be asking all along. Maybe it's in giving ourselves to that first question that we automatically fulfill the second!

So here I am today, thirty months until hand off! Our timeline has come into focus; selecting a successor is underway; important announcements to staff, leaders, and congregation await; my role as senior leader is subtly changing even now. And I'm okay with that! My energy level is up; my dreams for the future are bright, my hope for our church is firm. Because after all, the one who said, "I will build my church and the gates of hell will not prevail against it," is leading the way!

SECTION 3

For Couples Contemplating Transition

Denny Bellesi is one of "those guys" for me. You know the type I am talking about: the people God puts in your path to stoke a flame he lights deep inside of you. In my case, that fire is encouraging aging leaders in areas related to succession planning. Denny was one of the few older leaders who encouraged me, a thirty-something at the time, to keep pursuing this issue. I will be forever in his debt for the encouragement he extended to me.

Denny planted Coast Hills Community Church in 1985. In 2004 he and his wife, Leasa, made their shift from serving as founding leaders to their next season of influence. Back in 2014, I asked Denny to write down some things to encourage other couples that are preparing to go through a retirement-based transition. At the time, I posted this to my blog. His words are so practical I wanted to include them here as well.

A Letter from Denny Bellesi

Constructing a succession plan requires a significant amount of strategic and organizational thought. At its core, however, it is an extremely personal process. For example, in talking with leaders facing this issue, we have found that many find it challenging to initiate succession-focused conversations with their spouse. I think back to the many discussions I had with Leesa as we began to transition away from my role as a founding pastor. I started thinking, "If we could go back in time, what questions would we ask ourselves? Could we have done things differently so that our transition felt like more of a team effort?"

From that reflection came a series of questions Leesa and I recommend husbands and wives talk through as they navigate the succession planning process.

Six Questions Every Pastor Needs to Ask Their Spouse as They Prepare for a Succession

1. Do you agree it is time to prepare for our succession? If not, why not?
2. How can I honor you in this transition?
3. What would you like to accomplish before leaving?
4. What would it look like for us to "finish well?"
5. What would you like the next senior pastor and spouse to know about this church?
6. How can we dream together in a whole new way?

Five Questions Every Spouse Should Ask Themselves as They Prepare for a Succession

1. How will our children handle this transition?
2. How has the title of "senior pastor's spouse" shaped my life?
3. Am I ready to give up that title and that identity in the community?

4. Where will I get spiritual input during and after this transition?
5. Where will I call home?

Record your answers in a journal. Refer back to them often. Write specific prayers for one another. Jot down verses the Lord uses to speak to your heart. Respect one another's privacy by asking permission before sharing your conversations with others.

Above every other priority, fight for the health of one another's soul.

Denny Bellesi

SECTION 4

Recommended Next Steps

Thank you for investing the time, focus, and energy to get this far. As we conclude this leg of your journey, I want to offer a few practical next steps to consider:

Interview other ministry couples that have recently transitioned. Yes, there are horror stories related to retirement-based transitions, but let me assure you that healthy stories of transition are far more prevalent than you might think. Talk to these couples. Let their stories inspire and challenge you. I would be happy to connect you with someone if you need help.

Hire a coach or see a counselor. Hiring a coach or seeing a counselor can be an invaluable resource for you during the transition. They will help you process the personal side of succession while you work to help everyone else navigate the organizational side of things.

Engage with a consultant to help guide your planning process. Every ministry should engage the services of a strategic outsider that can help guide their succession *planning* process. They will not be blinded by the internal perspectives that can sometimes cloud a team's thinking. Strategic outsiders are also less susceptible to being overcome with emotion.

Here is a list of six areas I encourage ministry leaders to develop a plan for.

Protecting organizational continuity:
Anticipating and addressing potential areas that could be disruptive during a season of transition.

Transition strategy management:
Establishing a defined plan for how to manage the leadership transition process.

Communicating the transition effectively:
Communicating in such a way as to embed confidence in the process and continued investment in the ministry.

Proactive exit planning:
Helping a transitioning leader and their spouse prepare for their next season of influence.

New leader hiring:
Developing a profile, advertising the position, vetting candidates, negotiating the offer, and onboarding the successor.

Emergency transition management:
Writing a policy that guides the preparation for and response to an unplanned transition

Visit www.successionsherpa.com if you would like more information on how my experience with hundreds of leaders just like Jeff, Tim, Randy, James, and Cal can benefit you in your team prepare for transition.

APPENDIX: Additional Passages to Consider

Although the Bible doesn't include a "How To" section for succession planning, there are stories to learn from and principles to apply. Each of the passages below provides a unique lens through which to consider a transition. I have given a brief overview to help you get started, but don't let that be a substitute for digging into each text for yourself. This is not intended to be an exhaustive list of passages related to the broader topic of succession. I chose these because they serve as on-ramps to issues that tend to be overlooked in the typical planning process. May the Spirit of God use your time in the Word to give you much-needed insight and perspective.

A Prayer of Reflection – 1 Chronicles 29:10–19

Unlike Hezekiah, David's passion for the Lord burned bright to the very end. It is not the words of this prayer that make it unique; it is not so different than many other prayers of reflection that can be found throughout history. What makes this prayer special is the point in David's life at which he uttered it. Indeed, prayers offered at the end of one's life carry a particular, sacred weight.

A Request to Consider – 2 Samuel 21:15–18

After almost losing his life in battle, David's men told their aging king he would no longer be fighting on the front lines. They were concerned his diminished energy and strength would lead to his death. His men were willing to tell their leader he had become a liability in battle. Their motivation was respect and admiration, not a desire to get rid of him.

A Passion to Protect – 2 Kings 20:16–19

To truly appreciate this specific passage, you must read the full account in 2 Kings 18–21:9. Hezekiah's story stands as a profound example of how zeal and passion can diminish over time. At twenty-five he had the audacity to destroy the bronze serpent that Moses built some seven hundred years prior (2 Kings 18:4). By the end of his career, he was willing to trade Israel's future for his personal comfort. His zeal was gone.

A Lament to Wrestle With – Ecclesiastes 2:18–21

Solomon's concerns expressed in these verses have echoed through the hearts of leaders throughout history. It is understandable, natural even, that men and women who invest their lives in something would lament that someone else would eventually step into their shoes.

A Message to Deliver – 2 Peter

Peter wrote this letter with the awareness that his time was drawing near (2 Peter 1:14). In it, he distilled his wisdom and perspective into sixty-one verses spread out over three chapters. I think a leader with Peter's experience could have filled an entire bookshelf with insights and learnings. Perhaps there is something to be learned from his brevity and focus.

A Leader to Develop – 1 & 2 Timothy, Titus

Read these letters from the perspective that Paul is equipping his successors. Perhaps he feels a sense of urgency because he knows his time on earth is short. Or, Paul takes the idea of developing younger leaders seriously. Regardless of his motivation, you can sense how important it was to Paul to prepare these men to lead in his absence.

Printed in the United States
by Baker & Taylor Publisher Services